Odd Nest

poems by

Dom Fonce

Finishing Line Press
Georgetown, Kentucky

Odd Nest

Copyright © 2026 by Dom Fonce
ISBN 979-8-89990-372-4 First Edition
All rights reserved under International and Pan-American Copyright Conventions. No part of this book may be reproduced in any manner whatsoever without written permission from the publisher, except in the case of brief quotations embodied in critical articles and reviews.

Publisher: Leah Huete de Maines
Editor: Christen Kincaid
Cover Art: Valerie Williams
Author Photo: Sadie Volpe
Cover Design: Elizabeth Maines McCleavy

Order online: www.finishinglinepress.com
also available on amazon.com

Author inquiries and mail orders:
Finishing Line Press
PO Box 1626
Georgetown, Kentucky 40324
USA

Contents

Mosaic with Death Approaching 1
Who Need I Be? 2

Maiden

Yard Dance 5
Backyard Pet Cemetery 7
The Culvert 8
Song for the Wild Frog 9
Thumb Burial 11
Garden Dance 13
For Caterpillars 15
The Fair 17
Voice from Upstairs 18
At the African American Debutante Ball in Youngstown 19
Baptistry 20
Sock Hop Love Dance 21
Riding into Town 23
American Mosaic 25
Forest Dance 26
We Are Clacking Hormones 28
Sunday Mosaic 29

Mother

Baby Bump 33
Just Married 34
Mosaic with Divorce 36
For the Clergyman Who Refused Prayer: A Found Poem 37
First Day 39
For Chrissy 40
Sky Dance 41
The Building 43
Last American River Fire 44
Kaleidoscope Woman 45
Mechanical Horizon 47
For the Child I Couldn't Afford 48

Field Dance 49
Saturday Mosaic 50
Purse with Stones 51
Queen of the Airways 52
Uranium Glass 54
For Debbie 56

Wife

Summer Mosaic 61
Makeshift Museum 62
Killing the Man 63
Affair with Coffee Grounds 64
Ugly Numbers 65
Split 66
I Enter Fifty Cemeteries Looking for My Son 67
Remembrance Mosaic 68

Crone

For John 71
Standing Over the Great Serpent Mound, 2017 72
Seasonal Something 73
Daily Rituals 74
Girl with Hair Brighter than Light 75
Singing Bowl 76
Earning You 78
Circle Dance 79
Mosaic as Time Ends 81

Acknowledgments 82

*For and from Patricia, my grandmother.
Thank you for vulnerably building a persona with me.*

Mosaic with Death Approaching

May we slice? May we sit at the table? May we stare at each other? May we sip bowls of me? A black eye separates here and gone. Somewhere, a girl spins in a green field like a top. Dress fanned out. Hair wild. See her from a down-looking view. Fall into her. Closer. Closer. Into her pupil. This is my name. *Patricia*. Put it in your mouth. Swallow. On the shelf goes a doll. In the cellar goes a doll. In the attic goes a doll. You will forget each. You will move on. May we slice off this slab of me? Place it down. Slice. Place it down. Halve. Quarter. Eighth. Place it down.

In a dusty corner of a frozen house, your father is a ghost, pepper-tongued, spitting violent silence into the dark, alone. His anger is thrown at himself. A crow swallows a crow. Boar swallows boar. Buck swallows buck. Empty room swallows empty room. The eye parts. Veil opens. You won't find feathers in the yard. If one is there, you left it for yourself. John died and walked through the veil. You will walk through the veil. You walked to kindergarten by yourself every day. You walked the city blocks. Your brother was born dead. He could not walk. Then you were born and nobody was happy. Then you became a woman and nobody cared. Then you got pregnant young and everybody cared. By the bird bath goes a doll. Inside an owl's hollow goes a doll. Buried with a dog goes a doll.

You have finished. Have more. The orange fat risen to the top. Thick, waxy layer. Break through. Stir. Serve. There will be three men, but you will only love one. If you include your son, there will be four men. If you include your father, there will be five men. You will love half of him, but claim you loved him fully. Only after sixty, seventy, eighty years will you fully love yourself. The old house has a grandfather clock. Tick. Tick. Tick. When grandma walks through the door, it stops. When she leaves, it starts again. Some magic. Inherited magic. Magic in red pumps. Look out the window. See the moon. Three women belly-dance in the yard. Three more beat on drums. See flame roll into flame. Bouquets of gray hair. Gold chains rattle. Topaz earrings swing. Warm sweat beads. Hear the crackle. Smell the smoke, incense-sweet. Feel them smack the round goat skins. Feel their hips sway towards a center. The fire. Bare feet on coals. Three and three. Inching closer into each other. Rippling focal point. For a stunning moment, they are brightness eternal. Then they disappear.

Who Need I Be?

For a time, I wished
to be marginal—futile.
                This is liquid.

Two minds make the broth.
We sing and dance through
the phone, remembering who

we are, deciding who we
ought to be. I and I.
                Does it matter?

Legacy upon legacy—
era folds into era. Place
your voice on my tongue.

Place you finger on my
finger. The difference is
        minutia—reversible

as a coat of paint. Cup
your hand on my shoulder,
kiss my cheek.

Is any of this possible?
Will I—can I—make you proud?

Maiden

Yard Dance

Today, I am pecking. Filling
      trees with winter's
           pantry. A woman
   paints the bark white,
              leaves fallen
         into the muddy mix
            below. She talks

   of sunscald—Ohio's
        unstable weather: scorching,
            frozen,
        often in the same day. I flutter still,
needle-nosed, pack holes
        with marbles. I peek
through windows, supper-seek,
        suck water from hydrangeas.

                I am told
                    to be seen and not heard—father
                smokes from his pipe, mother scrubs
                    with yellow gloves—I reject this
     normalcy and disappear
        for moments. In the yard,
            I plunge for worms, stretch
        them out to see
           which is the longest.

   I dance in dull thrums—
        grass to branch
            to bush—drape
a thick worm on each
        browning corner.
                Away from city-sound,
        hollering and hubbub,
            I make my odd nest, teeming
        with crawlers. When they call
           me inside, a patch of sassafras,

                              dressed in golden red,
               sticks to my foot. I pluck it
                        from the carpet and
                              slide it softly
                                          under my pillow.

Backyard Pet Cemetery

One, two, three…
One, two, three—each grave is a sanctuary
underneath this life-giving tree;
We come here with fur
in our nails and dirt-scuffed
knees—these mounds
are Elysian, enshrined in birth-
root, entangled in Morning
Glory: We count to thirty-five, thirty-eight, then forty.

Are we selfish to collect you like strange stones?
You, still, stuck, quieted alone
and pulpy underneath some man's boot.
Is this not the least that could be done?

When we step here, we do so shoelessly, each toe
twined in grass—you—raking up
from a shadow we will never
feel. When we die, we will be scattered
and our temples will reach every lampless corner.

We sing in flutters from your hollow
throat, those forest-deep hums,
caws, and croaks that throng in damp
country air—We see carcass
and make essence in our back soil.
In circles, we surround you and dance
to the dead—*Down! Down with the distant*
traffic! Down to devastation! Down
to the damn boot! Down to death—though
you are gone, we still feel you breathing.

The Culvert

My sister is alone, but seldom lonely—streams
vein our fifty acres. After flooding, waters swell,
gathering forest dandruff, brown at first,

then crystal through passage. She watches acorns
float, builds boats from bur oak leaves and twigs,
sets them on a frigid journey. She tells me minnows

burrow from mud, wade in creeks after rain.
She follows them across the yard, down hills,
until they reach the culvert—a concrete mouth

hungering endlessly for earth-flow. She speaks life
into it, hearing the cacophony of voices rebound off
the darkness within. She says, *Water runs. The day*

it stops is the day we're doomed. Last week, a truck
swerved, flew into the ditch, blocking the surge.
Through her bedroom window, she heard the sounds

of crash break through. She tells me she was dredging
only minutes before, that her body would've been
splattered if she stayed—that a ghost's warning

landed fly-quiet in her ear—*Phyllis, go home.*
Now, she only explores under canopy, far away
from the manmade. I watch her chase the uncatchable,

as if a piece of her is bobbing along. But then she feels
the culvert's wideness nearing, halts, turns away. I mirror
her, refusing to go near it, fearing that she's telling the truth.

Song for the Wild Frog

                    We pinned you to a tree
          while the adults watched television—

your underside, the softest
        parts, yawning
                at our fingertips.

                We remembered the cartoons,
       the gross-out humor, the frog

             splayed open on
                      steel, and the kids, much older
                than ourselves, holding distaste and curiosity

          simultaneously in each eye—and we looked

at you, muscle
        trying to jump through skin,
                without pleasure, without humor,
                        without a sense of purpose at all,

              and we cut deeply down your belly.

In there, in you, was something
              new to my young, naïve mind—pain
      created by me.

                      You winced like a man
                        trapped in a fire, and we
            let you fall to the grass, ran back inside
                and hid in our rooms.

When we were called for supper, we ate our words instead,
                    and at night we sat underneath
                        our covers with flashlights—

            the ghost of you smeared on our walls.

                    In the morning, we collected you

    from the dirt, and held you tight,
                                like a lost toy.
             The brown earth ate our
hands as we scooped out a place for you.
        We called it the "Frog Spot" and, as play came,

            as seasons changed, our feet
     dodged your grave, as if it were a
                           landmine.

Thumb Burial

Grandpa tinkers on his Buick
while I roll in mud. The country

wind whisks around my face.
Humidity wisps bugs into my ears,

until all breath stones to a halt
with a scream: *God fucking dammit!*

Air speckles red in flight, the fresco
of factory men. On the floor,

his severed thumb dances.
Ba-dun ba-dun—the garage door

trembles, a mouth holding in a cough,
as his back bangs off every wall.

I don't know the sky from my own shirt.
Somewhere, in the dirt, it settles

and Grandpa calls, *Come here, girl!*
Come find this damn thing.

Then he runs in to stop the bleeding.
I dive to pick it up. The thumb has made

its home in cobwebs—I swear it moves.
I swear it wiggles as if it was speaking.

This is the first time I remember
almost holding his hand.

I think of Westerns, the Confederates,
the dynamite exploding, and I feel

my arm swing forward towards the grass.
Did you find it? he asks. I look out

into a backyard, toward a space,
I can never understand.

No. No. I couldn't find it anywhere.

Garden Dance

When I die, spread
               a little bit of me
                         in every garden. Leave me
      for the fairies. Heap me on mushroom
                         caps. Mix me
              through the pierogi flour, thumb

a hole in the mound,
     then plop the yellow egg
                  inside. Leave me
                         for the gnomes and the dragonflies.

             Cake me in mudpies.
                Run me through the wind.
                  Let me be
                        of the soil, the bee balm,
           the geranium, the goldenrod,
                     the marigold, indigo,
bark and root. Let me be
     a vein in the compost. Please,
                let me be anything
                        but locked away.

                *

          There's a lonely slash
     of sweetgrass
                in my front yard. Years ago,
a rip in the seed bag
         set a tail. I let their randomness
         grow from my garden.
         Doing this is easy—cultivating,
               maintaining, feeding, watering.

       I fork my fingers
                into ground to feel
                     its coolness. What's hard
                          is starting, cracking

                through plain soil, plotting
                    holes and painting
                            the housefront. A creator
    landscapes in her likeness,
                so on my seventh day,
                        I planted a ball of fire.

                            *

                Finally, I am uprooted—held
                    towards the sun
        by a young girl. She picks
                through all my layers, marvels
                        at my purples and blues.

            When she twirls, I twirl.
                            Time is meaningless.
    That's the beauty
            of losing control.

                    The sky folds over, starts
                            to rain. I'm tossed
                                into a puddle
                    as she runs away. Each droplet

                            pushes me lower
                                    and lower into thick
                    mud. Pure darkness
                            lasts only seconds. Sunshine
                                    nudges me. I open and see

                    the young girl whirling
                            in the yard. Leaving,
                                    returning, picking, twirling.

14

For Caterpillars

I am invisible, shirt stuffed
and undulating with tiny

disasters. The blisters bloom—
because I am young,

I must touch everything.
A man smokes a cigarette

across the field. When I see
him, I place the bristly

body between my fingers.
I remember coiling

with myself in the autumn
piles, bark-flavored,

red-brown seeping
into my jeans. I let them

freely roam my skin, make
home on my collar—I will

suffer tomorrow, but for today
I am happy being a nest.

If one falls from the horde,
it falls into the future.

My sister is in the house,
alone like me, only dartingly.

She sticks her teeth
in the windowsill's wood,

eyes jumping across the backyard,
better reading than a book—mouth

agape, hungering for a world
she has yet to discover.

The Fair

I have never become a town, though
the ghost-thought swimming in the streets
nips at my ears—never hammered
a city inside myself. As a child, I gathered

fairground buckeyes in my shirt,
like a drain hoarding marbles, and skipped
them off brick walls, morphing

tree orbs into moth wings
in my mind—to hope
something new would birth

from the debris below, to make
a collection multiply through explosion.

Yes, ants cluster around a molten dab of butter,

and will wage war to do so, but there is no
celebration in that. Here, we are crowds
smiling at crowds—occasionally wondering why

we are here and how respite zips at us
like flies. Perhaps wood and iron keep
a soul sparked from a child's first night being

one in thousands—seeing the adults
toddler-wobble in tow—and the quiet of empty
cornfields staring in from the outside.

Voice from Upstairs

Throughout the house, warm air rises
 and breaks with the Grand Canyon Suite

—sounds waking, running, walking—then Dad
switches to Hungarian Rhapsody No. 2.

Keys jump into my ears, place me on a stone ruin.
I'm climbing, clambering, conquering a foreign

crest. I'm filled with notes, buzzes, tings, strings:
each beat brings me into a future, uncut meadows,

red mountains, blue towers—pictures darting, hitting,
then departing. He switches again. The voice stands

in acapella, wavering, wobbling, whirling
from the 33 record—watery Soviet words fill each room.

I realize this is Grandma: I'm lost in tar. Her essence
splits through the strange language—language

that feels like dampened grass. The audio hisses, pops.
The ache from her lips passes to my bones, wanting

for a land that could no longer have her.
When we moved to the country from Cleveland,

something left my father's work-worn eyes, his boot
of a face—gathered up his mother's softness, inhaled

her in moments, captured her on vinyl for times,
I suppose, like these. I imagine him sinking

into his chair cushions, butter into bread. I shift
into a feathery blank, a future left floating

and misplaced. Her voice cuts a wailing height,
then dies: the house doused in quiet.

At the African American Debutante Ball in Youngstown

She folds
      underneath him—
           wrapped up like a family
                heirloom—and he holds
                      her hand as a father does
    to the back of his newborn.
The jazz musicians pause,
          inhale something more than air, and exhale
                    the Viennese Waltz. They all swing.

                Somewhere, a child twirls a dandelion
          between his fingers, stops, and blows white feathers
                into the sky—

now she is a castle of fabric and he
        is a guard dog watching
                the door. They step

        in neat handshakes, and the girls move
                from boy to boy and back
        with each beat.

                In the end, the hall simmers
                    to a halt—every girl has finally
    arrived; innocence has left
        each eye—the universe is placed
                down in portions

          to comb through and procure.

            They all choose, "Yes, I want it."

    And the room turns crimson, explodes with saxophone blasts—

                    quickly, they stuff their
          laurels down their gloves

                and set the room ablaze.

Baptistry
>   *after Amanda D. King*

My hem is undone—stitch
left dangling, sight unseamed.

Shake me awake. I scatter rust.
This is how I hide myself

from myself. You say I need
to bathe away my transgressions.

To your disappointment,
I dip my toe into the paint can

instead. A can that's dripping
off the shelf—a large "P" written

on the side. This "P" is for "pink"
is for "person" is for "plunge."

I fill the tub, fall in backwards,
my skin as slick as a mannequin's.

Your hand stops my full
submersion, my face from sinking.

I rise veneered in gloss—coated
in the color you don't want, but need.

Sock Hop Love Dance

I stuff Salisbury steak
        in my mouth, brain taxed and belly hungry—
              body twisting
      in skin—run with morsels

                        to the gym. In the center, shoes
              pile. Wandering awkwardly. Ready
      in a poodle skirt, flowing

            from me, waterfalling in mom-stitched
        fabric. I look at them:
Who will it be?   *To meet me sweaty palmed?*
                      To whirl out worry?
              To slip, rip, and fall with me?

        A boy, nerves jolting through his shoulders, blinks
to me, presents a momentous wash away.
                    We wait together

in silence,
      the record scratch over
                  loudspeaker—*Shake, Rattle, and Roll!*
    snakes the bleachers, nests
                in my ears. Smiles line
    the court. I am a ball of carefree, confident

        in fleeting seconds,
      then screw-faced and uncertain—I ask:

What is love?   *Am I doing it right?*
    What is lust?   *Am I doing anything right?*
What is my body when I'm home alone?   *When I see his face?*
                                When I think of him?
Why must I move?   *When his voice cuts through the*
                              music?
What is he saying?   *Something about me?*
                                Something about forever?
                                Something about
                                  letting go?

The bell rings: *Was it twenty minutes*
 already?—he sneaks a note, an invitation
 for more, to dance into a future
 that tilts just out of focus.

Riding into Town

A letter is placed
inside each girl's mailbox:
Class of '61 – Free Jewelry
Box for All Graduating Girls –

Karl's Jewelers,
Middlefield, Ohio.

After I find mine, I hide myself
on the Amish roads, ride my horse

into town—clomp-clomping past the culvert,
the ditches—along cornfields, homes dotting
acreage after acreage. My hair roams freely, crow

feathers spread against a front. Steel has taken
Dad to Cleveland. Mom is making the house.
I am left alone and unconsidered

in my daily duties—I could walk,
but what's the fun in that?

I want to feel the animal
under my hips, smile and nod
at strangers, young girls

who want to ranch. I want gnats nipping
at my face. I want to be candlelight
in a midnight meadow.

Downtown is small, masked
in old-American, signs swinging
above the sidewalk. I hitch her

to the building's side, run in. Soon, I saunter
back with my prize—bigger than I thought,
notched on the edges, ribbed down the sides,

dark brown wood. An evergreen-coated
mountain, with a winding river at the base,
is painted on the top. I ask, *What's the point
of an empty box?*

I imagine stuffing it
with acorns.
Maybe a small stone

from every road I walk on.
I imagine the ting of Grandma's sterling.
Maybe I will work at a tchotchke store

and hoard the statuettes, pins,
and magnets for myself.
The strawberry roan neighs

at a buzzing fly. The sky turns orange
over the rangeland. *Maybe I will fill it
with little moments.* I run my hand down

the mare, pinch a strand of her mane,
and pull. She doesn't flinch. I gather
a string of my own and zip it from my scalp.

I don't flinch either. I wrap them around
my finger. *Let's start here.* The box opens—
I see into its darkness, dangle our double helix

above—mother to a hatchling—then release.

American Mosaic

I am elbow-to-elbow with the other girls, FOR SALE hanging from my neck. Have me. Please crack me. I am rigid as glass. Smile in my face and tell me *you're the one I'm taking home.* Seersucker suit. A fly buzzes around syrup. Box trucks pull off at every curb, wooden ladders fastened to their spines. Please pack me in your pastel blue refrigerator, satin-sleek. Boys jangle silver. Jitter like Jerry Lewis. Flash me your teeth like Jerry Lewis. Oil your hair like Jerry Lewis. Veneer yourself like Jerry Lewis. Treat me like a flower in camera-flash. Grind my scraps down the disposal at home. Each girl enters a shop. Paint buckets fall from a scaffold, flooding the streets red. One-hundred flies entomb themselves in liquid sugar. Lick the lid of the cookie jar. Block me in slabs of gelatin. Scoop me like mayonnaise. Pick a chip of pastel from the refrigerator as the clock strikes noon. Smoke me like a carton of cigarettes. Burn me like a river. Dare to wear me like a rosary.

Forest Dance

Don't take this personally.
    When I consider tearing
        into a mother rabbit,
        I don't think of her litter—each kit
            crawling alone
                for creek water.

        I am action and reaction,
            an empty stomach
                and mouthfuls of indulgence.
      Past the trees are hills.
        Past the hills are rocks.
            At the rocks is an overlook.

This is where I stand,
    scanning down
        for movement. Maybe
            there's a cottage
                painted in the distance.
      Maybe I am circling
        a lost turkey. Maybe I do
            this just to remember
      nature claws in me.
                The moon looks
            like a face in flash-flicker.
        Maybe this is my face.
          I've been panting
              in the heat.
      I've been drooling
        in the dirt.
            I've been shaking
              in the cold. Maybe
we all need to let a scream loose.
        Maybe if you're the only one
      around to witness it, you can do anything you want.

So, I do.
      Howl. Say, *fuck you*
                    to the cottage, the comfort
of a roof. Say, I am what I want.

            Get down as low as I can,
                          still in the litterfall, waiting to snap.

We Are Clacking Hormones

You inside me is a vibration. In my pores. My cells. Two scoops melting into one. Curtains are black, pinned tightly shut. Bed jumps from carpet. House empty. Nobody taught us to do this: bitten ears, licked chins, tightened throats. We are so far from textbooks. I mirror elm in thunderstorm, sway on you. You mimic rockslide—the slow-then-fast shatter of gravity. I am shoes twisting on the dance floor. You are monster movie growl. I am heated glass dripping red. You are brick through factory window. I am water droplet on tongue. You are spit from a chide. I am poking-stick. You are worm in the apple. I am dancer on a single toe. You are car crash. I am drumbeat. You are hand. I am wrist. You are armpit. I am nail. You are fingerprint. I am my mother screaming at my father. You are father tearing the white gown. Silence. Violence. Cut. Blood. I am stressful smoking. You are match strike. Together, we are matchbox fallen from the counter, littering the floor.

Sunday Mosaic

A girl plays in a field, whistle-wailing to the woods. Leaves dress in decay. Nothing is happening. Paint us in bomber jackets. Let the bluebird go. Bury the BB gun in the backyard. Catch the white sheet of paper before the floor eats it. Dig yourself a hole. Stuff pockets with root beer candy. Call your friend. Fuck the boy from the mall. Blow Big League Chew. Blind yourself in neon swirl. Throw the ball back to the girl in the field. Toss a beer can into the sky. Ding it with a BB. Watch chocolate squares melt on your forearm, mud seep into the carpet. Nothing is happening. Braid grass clippings into a crown. Fight a parking lot shadow. Drop a bag of seeds. Step on your cat's tail. Gnaw on a plastic straw. Kiss your own hand. Send a baseball bat through your car's windshield. Watch a woman give birth. Peel a tiny sticker from a kiwi. Nothing is happening. Sit in the field as a girl disappears into the woods.

Mother

Baby Bump

You are welcomed weight, sponge in my midsection. Every day, I drop another bead of water onto you. I hid you like a bird in blankets for so long—now, I am an olive on a toothpick. I am sorry for everyone's unexpected cries, that this is not as joyful as it should be. And for Bob's yells echoing around my belly—Do this! Do that! Can I just *have* for once?

At the store, I am looking for a new lamp, something to hang on our new apartment wall. A woman says, *But you are so young!* I tell her I love my husband. She isn't convinced, pouts, and walks away. You are so heavy. My back is stiff and shooting pain. Then, you kick. I imagine my finger, a candlestick, dripping onto you again, your mass piling.

We are in the country, picking up a used couch from Bob's uncle. They do the lifting. I sneak away into the woods, their grunts becoming softer as I walk. I breathe in morning dew, run my hands along evergreens. Hoof-beats thud in the distance. Shrubs shake. Crows squawk then fly off. A flash of brown darts past me. Then another. Then another. A band of deer: fawn, doe, and buck.

He sees me, snorts anger from his nose—eyes turning bloodshot—does not want me there, bangs his antlers on a tree trunk. Kicks up dirt. Circles. Paces. Then, he charges. Gore surges through his mind. Closer. Closer. To tear into us—claw swiping skin. Closer. Closer. Closer. Then.

The doe cuts in front. He softens. Reluctantly turns away. We hold a glance that feels too long, as if we are speaking. In a cluster, she moves them deeper into the woods, as I move you back to the house. When I emerge, my feet return to field, you kick.

Just Married

I struggle onto the hospital's
    curb. Bob speeds
        his truck into the night,
            not glancing back—the warm
      August air steeps
          my skin. Numb, I carry
    us alone
        to the front desk, yellow fluid
dripping onto the floor,
        and try to say *I think my water broke.*
      Instead, my son gasps
        from inside me, swallows
            my words. I blur
  and mutter, *I thought this would be different.*
        The receptionist looks
at my stomach, then my face,
      with concern. I stare into a blank
            future, glide down
        the hall like a leaf
           in a gutter.
      The nurse sets me
        in a bed, asks for a name. *John.*
    No, your name. *Patricia.*
        Date of birth. *I'm 17.*
    I just got married.
           She sighs, slides the
           clipboard
    next to me. We're going
           to etherize you.
           Okay.
What is that? Don't worry.
    Just relax. *Okay.*
          She begins fluffing
            my pillow and tells
            me
      to get comfortable.
           Am I going to be a
           mother?

Her face sags, eyes
            rejecting mine. *Yes, dear,*
                        she says, then escapes
                                    to another room. Under
                                    lamplight,
            I begin laboring by myself.
My son rips for his freedom—
            I look over at the doorway, a young
                        bride frowning
                                    in at me. She walks in whispers
                        to my side, puts a hand on my shoulder.
                                    Like an animal on a spike,
                                                            I scream.

Mosaic with Divorce

I begin rationing. Boys play in the lot behind Phar-Mor. I slice each Steak-umm into smaller bites, then slice again. Today, the well water tastes like dirt. I ting coins of coffee tins, hang diapers out the window. I smoke around the baby. Cry around the baby. Scream at the walls around the baby. A light flickers above the stove. My mother tells me I will kill my father. When I can, I get lost alone in Strouss' Mall, bat my eyelashes for free malts. I will marry a poor man and we will be a poor couple. With the baby asleep, I wash dental floss to reuse the next day. A poor man sits behind Phar-Mor, squirts tobacco from his lips. At the gas pump, I lift the hose, dribble out the remainder like a mouth exorcising stress-vomit. If it looks alone, feels alone, sounds alone, it's probably alone. If I married a poor man, at least we wouldn't be alone. A boy falls and scrapes his knee. I spray the pan with Pam precisely so as to not overcoat it. I flip a fried egg. It disappears. Crack another one. Flip it. Vanish. In the dark, I bundle into blankets. Stuff everything I own into my mattress, hoping the pressure of my body will keep it from escaping.

For the Clergyman Who Refused Prayer: A Found Poem
Source: An angry letter

Dear Clergyman. Refused
prayer. Deny a lost lamb
to his flock. Jesus would
not look to pain. Pain
you have caused. Persecute.
On his deathbed. Husband.

Laughed with friends, fixed
the roof. Linda. Months
worrying for wellbeing.
Not worthy of prayer?
Perhaps you should look.
Look to your deathbed.

Look to your flock.
Look for Jesus. Surely
this was not
the Christian way.
(Father, Mother,
God, Goddess).

Forgive him.
Request for prayer.
Look to your Faith
for forgiveness.
Clergyman, Reverend,
Minister, Man of Cloth,

Servant of God. Worthy pain.
Think of Jesus
and Joseph. Hard work
and wood. The Husband.
Fixed the roof. Think
of Jesus on the roof.

The Husband on the roof.
Worthy of Faith
on the roof? Made
memories. Prayer
for the lost flock.
The Christian Way.

First Day

The Amish girl knocks on the door. Bonnet
and blue dress. Calls John just a *boppli—*
baby, she clarifies. Flashes funny faces

to him. He giggles. The apartment is plain-
walled, unlived in. I'm still hiding
my bruises. Every corner of her is beautiful

and handmade. She says, Y*ou know*
the way it is. I don't know. This is my first day
as a cash-clerk, divorce still on my collar.

First day of any job. *One for wash, one for wear,*
one for dress, and one for spare. Her way
is so cute—that I do know. She is a year

or two younger than me. I can't tell
if she's innocent or mature. I can't tell much
about me either when I stare into her. *I wore*

the one for dress today. I really need this job.
I understand. I have my best yellow shift
dress on. I want to be like Jackie. Want to forget.

Want to be seen. Want to show my healthy
arms. Want to show a little above the knees.
A light begins to flicker. Everything in here

should be brand new. It's too high for me
to reach. We let it be. I ask her, *So, do I*
look like Jackie? The Amish girl doesn't

understand. *I don't watch TV,* she says.
Of course. I leave ten dollars and head down
the hall, towards my way—John's little mouth

wailing for his mother through the wooden beams.

For Chrissy

I call you oracle—seer in the gray,
splitter of veils. I call you miracle.
We bore you from city to city, doctor

to doctor. They scanned a lump
within your head, called you malignant.
Rush. My back folded under

the weight of *this isn't supposed
to happen to us.* You were too young
to notice, picking dandelions

on the hospital's lawn. Just, *I can't see
good, Mommy.* They placed your body
into tubes, lasers beaming

through you—needles into a pin
cushion. We waited. Bit our knuckles
raw in the sterile fluorescence. Second

opinion. Benign. Only blind. What consolation.
They tried everything. Patch the good
eye so the bad one grows stronger.

Fail. You lived in milky white for years.
You learned how to dance, how to play—
somersault, catch the ball, throw, kick,

fight, ride, twirl—in the milky white.
You mothered in the milky white.
Worked in the milky white. Grieved

in the milky white. Only there could I
understand your point of view,
blind in loss. And how I learned

to run back into the comfort of clarity,
away from your reality: a space
I'm not brave enough to withstand.

Sky Dance

The air licks my face, a droplet
                on tall grass. I am up, beyond
     ground-sight, floating
                    in flocks, hovering alone,
                              steeple-perched when it pleases me,

        watcher from a high window.
            I know I know this much:
                      sticking a foot in mud
            is a chore. In the sky, I am
        fine being hungry—along
                  the clouds, I feel nothing,
              am reaction poured into body—here,

I exist in an every-view.
        I sit on a limb, spot a child
                gulping soup
        from his bowl.
                When he looks at me,
he runs to the glass, and pats
        on it. Then, I am gone.
                I flash down a river,
                pluck a silver-blue fish

from the water.
            When I bring it home,
      my children wonder
               how I found one so fresh.

                At night,
          as our home snores, I sneak
                  out into dark, shout
            my plea from a heartwood
            hollow—

       the air listens, coos back,
                chirps, croaks, fiddles
                          a message:

every dream starts
            with a leap,
and you are on the edge
                of a world.

The Building

There's a memory or two stuck on this floor—crowds standing on crowds, vendors waving their wares. In a forgotten minute, a girl teethes on her mother's collar, hides in her breast, as women fight over the latest fabric. The smile will surface, strong and even—and she will grow to endure loud noises, a green light swinging above a street. Only the ghosts bounce off these walls—there's no more Strouss' malts and malls and makeup stands—just offices and phone calls and the echoes of fraud. The building's bones chatter—the city's stomach blazes in the basement, its voice whirling from the mezzanine and balconies, horizon sparking the skyline. The difference between building and body lies within a squint. In the crack of a brick, the ground swells—each beam, each weld, each windowpane shifts, breaks. One-thousand arms for one-thousand lost thoughts reach out, grabbing something pretending to be promise.

Last American River Fire

Man tilts barrel into river—chartreuse swirls
the murk. We are entering the city, Elvis

on the radio, the kids peeking over the bridge
as we pass. In Cleveland, we see Grandma,

go to "Russian" church, sip cold bowls of borscht.
Afterwards, we lie, lazy bundles around the TV.

Sirens sing wee-woo in the distance. This city-sound
is expected, until the newsman's demeanor solemns.

The camera shows smokestacks rising
from the Cuyahoga, eating the sun. John dashes

to the window, then shoves it closed. He says,
There's a monster coming right at us. We all rush

out the front door to see—black clouds stare,
the face of God in each rolling plume, mouth

stretched inhumanly wide. We are crumbs
in its wake. I gather the kids underneath me.

The doorhandle sucks from my grasp, bangs
against the siding. *Wee-woo! Wee-woo!* Each family

lines the sidewalk. Pure curiosity. The toxic wall
snatches more and more clean air. When it takes

our block, it takes us—lungs burn in sky-char—I dig
my nails into the wood, strain every fiber, and slam

the door closed. The sirens cease. The newsman says,
Emergency workers have the fire under control.

There's no need to worry. I look at my children,
hold each hand, and know he's lying.

Kaleidoscope Woman

Mold me into multiplicity—make
a good woman, a witch, a wretch—

build me sexy in one flash, ugly
in another. I am a mother.

This cannot be undone. It's easy
to raid closets, pluck a skirt, conceal

a hat. In the city, it's easy being anyone.
Where I live, so small every schoolboy

has kissed every schoolgirl, I am
eccentric. I wear feathers, huge

pashmina scarfs, high socks striped
with black and green. I drive

the school bus. Here, I go unjudged.
In my pointed hat and cape, I cast

spells on the children. They giggle
and wave twig-wands in return.

I tell them, *Do no harm with power
so strong. Wish for only good things.*

I don't know their peace, their tumult.
When they say, *Yes, Mrs. Neil*, I believe

them. In the bedroom, I sprout bunny
ears, negligée, tall boots. My husband

isn't interested. I exhale, flop down next
to him. As a side job, I'm called out

to play a balloon-a-gram nurse, embarrass
men on their birthdays—the art

of look-but-don't-touch. The drunk
men see me as they see a pin-up calendar,

but at least they look. I am decorated
in red lipstick and white stockings, a cross

on my chest—check their temperatures.
He bites down on the thermometer.

His buddy bites on his own finger.
All the women roll their eyes.

I can't help myself and bend down
with a smirk, kiss him.

Mechanical Horizon

My children are unruly, but I see
this as a good thing. In the laundromat,

boredom eats them, enchanted by swirls
and grumbling machines, flashing lights

and buzzes in the air. Other children
are unhappy and well-behaved. I let mine

touch everything. In the aisles, they push
each other in silver laundry carts. I see

Debbie's little brown head, Chrissy
and John's gold, bump along

this mechanical horizon. When one falls,
scuffs a knee, the crying is muzzled quickly.

Each sibling corrects the other, shushes,
assuring this is fun. At our final beep,

I fold extra slowly, wait for the cart
to reach my aisle. Just before they pass

me, smiles wide as a town, I push hard
on John's back, propelling them on dangerous

speeds they could only dream of,
only a mother could produce.

For the Child I Couldn't Afford

There's an imp perched on my bare shoulder—bumpy skin, teeth long as greedy fingers. Yellow guilt oozes from him, perplexing guilt, guilt for not feeling guilty. There's a nest in my hands. This nest holds three eggs. A fourth would topple us all. The imp isn't interested in reason. He snarls at my neck. When I sleep, he flies throughout the town tilting every glare towards me. I should be shivering in judgement, but I'm not. With my children cozy in their beds, I'm cozy in mine. The imp asks, *What does that make of you?* I'm answerless. Wouldn't it be easier to hate myself? To stew on selfishness? To hold my breath in a bath of self-loathing? But I don't want to.

I want time for time to pass. I want space for my children to take more space. I want growth to grow from what has already blossomed. The imp claws blood from my muscle, trying to twist out a guilt I don't have. I wrap my naked body in a cloak of my choosing. When the imp speaks, his words trickle to the ground. When he licks, tasting for my sweaty skin, he's aimless. He sniffs. Growls from the gut. I am invisible. He leaps off, flies away to pester some other woman. I should be guilty for not having you, child I couldn't afford. Could I have stretched the fibers of this nest to fit four? Surely, I should be guilty for not trying. But I'm not.

Oh, child that I couldn't afford, you were just not meant to be.

Field Dance

I'm in the golden field, draped
                in honey straw. Watch me
                      gallop. Watch me bow, chomp
      at the ground—with this much air,
                I can be unruly. In the cramped corners

      of my room, I'm as slow
            as larva. But, here,
I become stomp.
        I am rustle.

                When a fly lands
                      on my eye, I shake
        it free—it circles
                upward into the swirling
                      center of a cloud. Rain
                    comes. Let it.

Each fiber in my legs: fire.
        I'm fine treating my hands
    as hooves, sewing a tail
              to back the of my jeans.
                  These moments
of aloneness are fleeting,
        must be stolen: lunchbreaks,
                while the kids are napping,

    the reason why I took so long.

            I gather a bundle of tall grass,
                  coil it, then take a bite.

                I'm not sure it will digest.
                    I'm not sure I want it
                          to.

Saturday Mosaic

Dice yourself into twenty-eight cubes. Open a nesting doll. Open a nesting doll. Open a nesting doll. Simmer in a pan. Boil in a pot. Become garnet. Father ivory. Mother emerald. Sister silver. Stir. This is a peck of dill. Flick mud off your toe. Recalibrate. Resettle. Find a church just outside the city. Feel the black of your hair. This is a potato. Cut off a root. Shave off the dirt. Without this, we would starve. Open a nesting doll. Open five bags of seed. Feed five crows. Dive into a pink pond. Stir. Find faces in painted eggs. When you leave, wrap your head first. When the rainwater trickles from the rusted shed, drink. It should be this bright. Mix with cream. Drop an egg into the creek. Watch minnows try to swallow it whole. Poke a dead coyote with a stick. Bury the stick. Burn the body. Your father will call. You will run into a wall of kudzu. Open your sister. Watch yourself sleep inside. If you wake yourself, you will scream. Hug your father. Understand that things only last if you help them along. Read twelve books. Sing twelve songs. Dance with your neighbors. Understand cutting like this will protect your fingers. It will smell like nothing. Taste like nothing. That's how you know it's done right. A cube falls from a spoon. Dig to find it. Find a pea instead. Hide it within the core of every nesting doll. Hope your grandson finds it one day. Serve cold.

Purse with Stones

In the city, I disguise myself as an important woman—
purse thick with necessity. I must be a traveling

woman, must look interested. I need a bottle for this. A prescription
for that. A palette and mirror clamshell. A checkbook. An army

of loose change. But these lumps click as I walk. Someone asks,
what's clacking in your purse. Quickly, I talk about the weather.

I go on with my day, plant one on a road, one around my neck,
one deep in the woods, one in my pocket. Find one in red,

one in swirls, one layered in gold, one shimmering black. I see
a calico stone. It speaks. I crack open my purse. *I've seen five*

pairs of lovers, twelve scraped knees, a boy with a slingshot
picking birds off trees, and a single murder. I believe it. I reach

into my purse's mouth, remove a glittery Colorado geode
from inside, place it on Ohio dirt. At home, I write notes

to my husband, hide them in jars, then the jars in junk drawer
he will never open: *When I die, place a stone in my stomach*

for every year I've survived. Set me on a boulder then a boulder
on me, and so on, until we become eternity. I climb into bed,

outline myself with each new stone, each dully humming
a story I am too tethered to tell.

Queen of the Airways

is what all four crown me—husband,
son, daughter, daughter—ditzy
and dancing in the mundane. I'd rather

be embarrassing than boring, inappropriate
than a stitch on a lip: why can't I ask
questions to everyone about everything?

The kids rile me up for laughs, say,
Yell over to that homeless man. I do it
because I'm not afraid to. I do it

because it's unbecoming. Sometimes,
I forget things on purpose—leave
the pasta underneath the cart, have to drive

back to find it. They say, *Our Sunday is ruined.*
I say, *Now, our Sunday is an adventure.*
They throw their hands in the air, make me

go alone. I relish it. There's a bus stop in front
of the store. I give a man a nickel, tell him
I'm a billionaire just to see his face. I walk

to every cart, make a scene, ask strangers
if they've spotted a blue box of macaroni.
Of course, it's already gone. Inside, I look

at this and that. Take my time. Try to forget
where the aisle is. I buy a blue box of Act II
instead. When I get home, they scold me

even more. I say, *Oh! I can't believe
I grabbed the wrong thing!* They roll
their eyes. We make grilled cheese

instead. When night sends everyone
to bed, I blink from my sheets, to the living
room. The TV is silent. Some western

is playing. I fill my mouth with mounds
of popcorn, happily allow a few kernels
to fall through a crack in the sofa.

Uranium Glass

A cough thunders
in my throat.
My house under
blacklight—every

smudge of me
on display.
On the walls,
shelves.

On the shelves,
iridescent dishes.
One for every day
of the year. Entomb me

in formaldehyde.
Steep me in brine.
Display my nakedness.
Remember I wasn't

afraid. I break a wine
glass. Hand a shard
to my daughter.
My invitation

to the odd.
A cough takes over
me. A living room
decays without

a little risk.
Some try rearranging
furniture. Polka dot curtains.
Wine sofa covers.

I place this room
in a square, in some row,
on some column
of danger. In the yard,

I filled my stomach
with fireflies. My father
purged them from me,
then locked me away.
Now, the Geiger counter
clicks the night awake.
My neighbors are surely worried.
If you paint me, color me

neon green. If staring too
long at the sun blinds me,
I will dance in moonlight.
I am becoming nothing

but a cough.
A proud, little cough.
This is me sipping
the hemlock.

For Debbie

Debbie's brown head flashes. She screams
in front of me. I fire down on the brakes.

I'm raised so high in the driver's seat I can see
blocks down the road. I nearly flatten her.

She climbs the bus steps and sits behind me,
five minutes late after class. Her eyes catch

mine in the rearview mirror, hold fear. I turn
up the speakers, the cassette plays Pink Floyd's

"Don't Leave Me Now." I spend the drive thinking
of abandonment—*surely, I thought she was*

already on or was I just okay with her walking home?
It isn't a long walk. When our eyes meet again, I'm sure

neither of us know. After I drop the town's children
off, only three remain in the cab: mine.

Twelve-year-old Debbie. Chrissy, fourteen. John, sixteen.
I try to pull out a mother's truism from deep inside,

but can't. I say, *I'm sorry for almost hitting you, Debbie.*
I'm sorry for almost leaving you behind. She nods.

I gather them inside the house to make supper.
Three years later, John has graduated. Chrissy

has softball practice. Debbie sits behind me,
occasionally making faces through the rearview.

We travel our regular route, each child gets off
at their normal stops. I wave to them. Sometimes

to their parents. Direct them across intersections
if they need it. Until just myself and my daughter

remain. But something changes my day. I look at her
buried in a book. She looks like me. She's looking

like a woman. I ask her, *Do you want to drive?*
I sense her entire body perk up. *Really?* she asks.
I nod. She walks to my seat, then sits in it. I direct
her eyes to every mirror, hands to every switch, button,

and lever, feet to each pedal. Her cheeks bright red
with excitement. She presses down on the gas.

The tires crunch gravel. Soon, she is sailing us
down a long, flat backroad, into the sun. I palm

down the horn. She does it next. Only the country
air can hear us, judge us. We're going so fast,

the chassis floats. Arrow towards apple. Dart towards
board. She is electric. She burns with newness. Every

little fresh sensation blazes from her eyes. We break
through a thick layer. Then I stop her only because I have to,

placing my hand on her arm. Take back control. Steer
us into the expected. The typical, though now slightly

skewed. I hit every pothole on the way home
to remind our bellies what flight feels like.

Wife

Summer Mosaic

Stamp picnic blankets with stones. Sun beating down on the table spread. Food in backroad air. Deviled eggs. Burgers. Macaroni and cheese. Almost step on a praying mantis. A boy. Hands clawed, stressed wide. Stretched pink in clutch. Climbing our home's gutter. Grunt with squirrel-chitter. A horsefly buzzes. Sweat drops from his ear. He's impressed with himself. Smile. Is that my son? I yell. Everyone yells. *Get down from there!* The yard, vast green, humidity-thick. My husband trucks a rusty pontoon. Figure eights. Grass spitting from his tires. Girls, my daughters, leaning from the bow. Slam the breaks. Soar to the front. Smile. Whip mayo in the potato bowl. Sprinkle chives from the garden. Grab the big, yellow spoon. A baby cries. A pair of cardinals flash in a bush. Beer in metal buckets. Slice the pie. Almost step on a frog. Throw a baseball. Press down tightly. Spray your sister with the hose. A child strips, runs around naked. Scoop him. Smile. Bring him inside. Blue. Orange. Pomegranate. Wine. Watch the night take the sky. Watch them all leave, cluster by cluster. See the yard alone in darkness. Sit on a stack of picnic blankets. Finally catch your breath.

Makeshift Museum

Today is for tidying—our home is dust-covered, lived-in. I spray the front window in lemon water, its panel as big as the floor, wipe it free of grime. I spend hours scrubbing the walls and everything they hold—antique rifles from the 1800s, Mardi Gras masks from 1989, peacock feathers from the 2000s, bull's horns, quartz-encrusted geodes, travel tokens, treasures from each coast and the flyover. Light on my feet, I twirl to pop music, loosen the cobwebs from each hangable, bookshelf, and blind spot. In the basement, I clean the jukebox, sweep the bison pelt blanket, look at the crystal scales of the rattlesnake skin.

A house must shed itself too. I bump a Peruvian pot. It shatters. Now, the house has lost a facet, doesn't shine like it used to. A small piece lodges itself in a cement crack, refusing to leave. Fine. This is what builds character. Because I have added to the mess, I move much faster—make the beds, fold the towels, shine the mirrors—turn the house into a curio cabinet.

When family arrives, they aren't brightened by my hard work. This is, and always has been, *Grandma's house*. Their eyes glaze over my new additions, careful preparations. When friends come over, they say, *Well, isn't that neat?* then change the topic. But, when a new guest arrives, they are greeted by my makeshift museum. When Rip brings them to the kitchen, I buzz in their ears, snag them in stories about this and that adventure. I smile with a thin layer of rehearsal and theatrics, tour them through the life of a woman who wants to be seen.

Killing the Man

I hold myself within a black oak box, no wider than a pin. From beneath his

pillow, I sneak it from my husband and ship it to another man. Inside the echo

of a dream, my husband watches me dance in a shallow puddle pooling on

this other man's tongue. Then he wakes up drowning in himself. He checks the

mail and listens to the line—notes every new crick in the movement of my

spine. There, he hears us cooing love songs underneath our breath and

watches warmth I once gave him vanish from my breast. He screams *I'll*

kill him, kill him, kill him! He snatches the shotgun, keys to the red truck. I cry

for him to stay, as the ides meet us in the heat of May, and the blazing sky

turns over. As the engine revs and his mouth spits bullets, I lay my body out

like a fallen branch, nose touching the tire's tread. After he cuts the ignition,

he comes to me, sobbing in my neck, and there I return my black oak box to

his shirt's front pocket, remake this empty house into an empty home

just as everyone expects.

Affair with Coffee Grounds

I stare into black specks, bone-white cup—first, I hope to see your face, an omen of twisted time, the rearranging of my universe, another divorce, another marriage. Then, I remember your face can't be there. I am only looking for simple things: hats, scythes, birds, balloons, pears. Instead, at the bottom, I see a maelstrom.

I move from kitchen to sofa, kiss my husband's earlobe too long. Imagine he's you, Rip. My daughter snickers at our over-affection, *So who's having the affair?* We blush, swerve the topic—ask if she's gotten an oil change recently. I track her, watch her enter the bathroom, wait for her outside and say, *I am.* She's red-cheeked, then walks away.

I look into the cup. Near the handle, I see lovers nuzzling in a cave. One is bleeding from the heel. I imagine us fucking in a car, nothing but bullfrog-croak fills the night—we are silent as teenagers, afraid to get caught. I can't handle it, scratch your back. You scream. I see blood in my fingernails.

On the front rim, where my lips leave a mark, I see a woman on fire—or causing a fire. I can't tell. She is on a mountain, high within the clouds, an aura blazing around her. I become the gas can in the garage, the matchbox strike, shedding old skin, the air burning around my mouth, unable to breathe. My first tantrum—my fiery foot kicking down a front door.

Ugly Numbers

I go to a party, tell a stranger I'm in love just to feel the words in my mouth again. When a woman gets divorced after an affair is she single or dating? I'm not used to saying love. Of course, Rip wants to get married. *I don't know just yet.*

I tell him four is such an ugly number: *If we marry, you'll be my third, which means forever.* He tells me of his love for summer camp, never being bored. *We can paint our property how we choose.* Archery here. Volleyball there. Swimming somewhere in the middle.

He's very convincing. I think of the children, grandchildren, and their children. See men within men. Women within women. I stall my *Yes,* count every number I can think of. I remember us in a bar, only a week ago, a woman whispering into his ear as I stood to the side. One jealous moment too many, at least for now. *No, not yet,* leaves my lips. He nods, kisses me on the cheek, and flips to channel three.

Split

I wake up. My hand grabs the sharpie. Draws a black line down, scalp to clitoris. Swaths my right side in red, left in green—my nakedness in the mirror. Paints down the chest. Clavicle in green and red. Breasts in green and red. Nipples in green and red. Down. Down. Navel caked in color. Hips. Buttocks. Under each cheek. Vulva. My pubic hair. Down. Inner thigh. Knees. Ankles. Feet. Then I dress.

Wind chooses color prominence. Dominance. In green, I'm barefoot in the grass—find faces of loved ones in bark—let ants climb my finger. In red, I'll set the day aflame—kick in the cabinets—scream at the dogs. Flowing clothes. Face left in the open. Rip gives me a kiss. Leaves for work. I call my sister. She doesn't answer. I go to call my daughter, but stop. I get in the car, drive to the flea market.

With the window down, the green chips from me, glitters in the air. Today has chosen red. Today may become a housefire. A man with a horseshoe of hair asks me if I have children. I tell him I ate them all.

He eyes me, twists his face, then leaves. I buy a Raggedy Ann doll. Plan to steep it with the spirt of my mother. Leave it in the backseat instead. I take a coffee mug into the yard. Launch it at a tree. Collect stones and throw them at the birdhouse. I haven't kept track of time. Rip sees me from the doorway. Knows me well enough to know what to do. Tucks me in bed like a toddler. For the best. My dreams swirl in green. I twist and turn. Red sheds from my skin until I'm sweaty and bare. In the morning, I wake up. My hand grabs the sharpie.

I Enter Fifty Cemeteries Looking for My Son

I bring your daughter, too young to grieve, to your grave. We paint your stone with *I Love You* words, *I Miss You* words, eat egg salad sandwiches in the grass, on top of strangers—I hear their voices bellowing below. The sun dances on our faces. Beetles crawl on our legs. We make a normal day into a great day.

We sleep. In a dream, I enter fifty cemeteries alone. My arms spread, the sky charcoal dust, and I am running between each plot—each soul tells me their histories: Vietnam War veteran, trophy wife, child with tuberculosis, firefighter, death row inmate. It goes on until the forest in the back touches my nose. In another dream, you never died, but I can't picture it well.

In wish alone, I am alone by your side. You say, *I forgive you*. I say, *I must be a horrible mother*. You say, *No*. This is how you lived. This is how I choose to remember you. I have the pedal to your Indian motorcycle in my pocket. I place it where your feet must be.

Remembrance Mosaic

Remember you rode the horse. Remember your daughters. Bobbing together. Blonde and brunette. They, too, rode their horses. Remember John. His daughter rode her horse. Frost glazes the windows. Hot breath on glass. Try to erase ice. Remember you twirled the dandelion. Remember a kissing bug zigzagged into your mouth. You swallowed. Remember the gulp felt right. Trees naked. Buried in snow. Gnarled fingers on pearly sheets. Maybe a deathbed. Remember there's grass. Deep underground. It begs upward. Remember the roly-polies. The worms. Beak in mud. Pluck. The beetles. Bumblebees. Skippers. Monarchs. Remember they live. Dormant. You must be dormant now. This is necessary decay. Somewhere children smile. Throw balls of white. Make forts. Make joyful days. Remember nothing is all bad. Barefoot on shag. Remember the yard lives. Close your eyes. Remember. For your sake, remember and allow time to spin.

Crone

For John

The labyrinth's belly burns in the dark distance—reddening muffled, faint through shrubbery—purring alive. Into the unknown, I bear you again, my son, in hand-jotted notes, sweep my arms across green walls, guided by candlelight. A man treks far in front, a woman slowly behind, and so on. My feelings sit in my hands, in these notes—I sift through and see *For John, For John, For John*. I've forgotten how many I've written: lifetime's worth of words in a world of *maybe one day*.

But I do not want to wait. I've seen you scurry behind the tree in our backyard, smoke cigarettes in the garage. You look at me, smile, then run just out of sight. *Oh, will you stay. I love you. Haunt me.* But I cannot force the universe to break for me—to see you, speak to you again, would only be a gift the universe gives. I haven't earned its generosity. I haven't sacrificed at the pyre of forgiveness. Blame begets blame becomes blame brings on more blame. *John, you are my son,*

and you have died. That is that. As I usher you forward, the galactic center of this journey brightens. I can nearly see it now—perhaps as you saw as you exited my womb—a fire big as a sun. I am at the edge now, so bright I begin to sweat. I feel you in my chest, son, drop each memory of you into the flame. Each note turns to ash, air. You remake me into everything.

Standing Over the Great Serpent Mound, 2017

I breathe deep, and in the
                      distance, hear the chug-pop
          of a John Deere,
               tall and green like corn stalks,
     and the walks
           of bumpkin lovers through the fields,

              hand-in-hand,
                         lip-on-lip,

                                    thigh-to-thigh.
They say, "I never want to leave this moment"—
                  twisting and rolling in dirt, fused
                            in roots, twined in grass.

                      I smell the oil on the mechanic's cheek,
crackle-rising smoke in the coal-lit factories—
                  taste brow-sweat the artist leaks down her
          face, and feel her lonesome stomach burble, as eyes
                        focus on work and only that.
The air is communal,
           transcendent; time
                  is torn and space is singular—each of one
                          body,
          everybody carving a great serpent—
   curving through unknowns,
            absorbing mysteries by mouthfuls—
   in their own eyes, on their own land, soft like blocked lard.

Seasonal Something

We escaped the electroshock era. I know a man who knows a mother that had everything stripped through lobotomy, personality and all. For us, it has only taken 60, 70 years to figure out how to be sisters. Remember, five years ago, we rented a cabin, sweated out decades of anger, resentment, together? We set everything down on the long, oak table, didn't throw a punch. Something about Dad blaming me for every hardship, something about October or November.

When the weather changed, so did our demeanors—wrathful, frozen, nippy. One winter, you threw a croquet ball at my eye. With that smack, you broke loose, my sister again, and placed my body on the couch, an icebag on my swelling. You cried real guilt. I felt that.

Now, we know our limitations. It is better that the family not see us on Christmas Day. Better to see them in January for *Russian Christmas*. The cold will have bitten us by then, our moods will have dipped, our husbands will have understood, and we will have been merry again. Sister, I am glad to understand you, as you helped me understand myself—something we all seem to lose, regain, through time—these flowers we fought to nourish, gone into their beds and back out again.

Daily Rituals

I face a Goddess in the East who wakes me: this is why I'm barefoot, harvest in heart. I count in threes, greet my reflection, ornament my fingers in turquoise and lapis lazuli—feel into my daughters, their children, their heartbeats, their worries. The day dared to crack this morning—this is why I glide to the front yard, why I shoot arrows at the sunrise, eat blueberries from the vine, draw circles of protection with my eyes.

If I am standing, Isis surges through my legs. If I sit, a brightness pools at the crown of my skull, then I push it down, down, down into the dirt. If the weather grays, I build barriers around the house. If a groundhog waddles past, I speak to it. If a bird lands by, it knows that it is I who landed beside it. If the wind whistles, I pat on my knees. If my husband leaves, I say, *goodbye* and *I love you*. If a neighbor laughs, I laugh at how preposterous this all feels. If a carcass is picked clean by crows, it is necessary.

If a buck gores another, it is correct. If a fox flickers in the cornfields, and starves alone, its fire still spreads furiously. If a hatchling falls, it is eaten by a loving earth. If a child dies just over the horizon, he knows what I know—these are just moments and moments and moments—I hold you with me, and you, and you, and

Girl with Hair Brighter than Light

When asked about my life, I give up the exciting parts easily. When I am asked something difficult, I become difficult. My throat knots. I remember my bad hip. My loosening thoughts. I remember a door was closed and I locked it.

Just a month ago, I was travelling. I watched a girl, a blade of grass riding a stream, playing in a yard. Her blonde hair ate the sun, was brighter than light. I tried running out of my skin, but couldn't, was stuck in my chair. When the girl saw me, she came close, asked, *How old are you?*

I said, *Old enough to stop remembering.* She didn't understand, told me she was eight, and moved on. Then she played, played, played, while I twirled a dandelion between my fingers. She summersaulted behind a house, just past my vision. I cricked my head from the shade, flexed my hips to follow. Looked up, whispered to the sun as if some god, and said, *Please take it easy on me.*

Singing Bowl

In the circle, we sit
        cross-legged, bunch up
                our pants to place skin to grass.
                        An ant dots
                                around my foot—I lose track
            of him, let bother leave me
                    in exhales. Strangers face
                          the center in every direction,
                    towards a woman, voice stretchy
                              with sweet-sound, as she taps

        a rod to the lip
            of a crystal bowl, slowly
                    gliding around and around.
                Sealing sunlight
                          from our eyes, we follow her—

our road warbles, each bowl
        breaks noise-knowing.
                      The air fills with heartbeat
              flutter, Babel-hum. Everything
                      in a moment, then nothing,

in waves. Everything. Nothing.
                Arms like pistons. Second passes second.
        Saturation in now. Sweat rallying
            from pores.
                Wom-wom-wom.
                        Water-beads thumping
            on a chest. Black hole
        swirling technicolor.
                Through time. In line. Space

                            tearing. Ears ringing.
                      Bodies floating, shuddering.

          I feel like a bag of perfect.
                   Shift. Zigzag. Buried
in a loving grave. Breathe the wind
      of others. Inhale. Within. Without.
                     Wom-wom-wom.

                          I am a dragonfly marsh-darting.
    A pond skimmer
        at the threshold. Eyes roll
back. Forward. Left is right.
      Right is up. An egg cracks.
            She speaks. We open.
One-hundred blackbirds
      watch us
                from the branches above.

Earning You

I mouth the words I wish I'd said to you. When
I see the yard filled with flowers and feathers, I
know you heard. I finger your name on bark.
You materialize, my son, to stare at me,
voicelessly, your face still and enough. Pale like
a man carved from soap. Every day, I sacrifice
my goat of an ego, try to understand the universe
is good in every decision. Every day, you arrive.
You are self-work surfacing. A tower I break and
rebuild from sunrise to sunset. The rabbit I
finally catch. When I close my eyes, you leave. I
walk the greenery, water slowly the sprouting
foxglove. A hawk lands in our tree, spreads
itself, then wings off. An earthworm inches
deeper into the dirt. A beetle lands on my
shoulder. I take off my shoes and sit in the grass.
My skin eats the sun, lungs inhale the clouds,
ears gather chirping. This is not greed, but due.
This is how I earn you.

Circle Dance

Women engrave me in mossy stone, soak rags—
pat me in portions, extract the weight of bruising

and bygone from my face, arms, legs, back, heels.
The circle caws within the tall grass, together

as one woman, striking drums, flittering
tongues, sweat-coated as the fire roars.

Goddess! Goddess! Goddess! fills the air—
the clouds roll over *Maiden! Mother! Crone!*

I'm whisked through wicker—into sisterhood.
I turn towards the circle. They jitter so softly,

nearly fluttering off the ground. I've arrived
in pale skin, thin tapestry dress, bare feet
and am titled *woman who holds her blood.*

My thighs flex. I do not force them.
My shoulders shake. I am not in control.
The sun ducks the horizon, and the moon,

bright as three stars, illuminates the field.
An effigy builds itself from coals, woman
as inferno, shambling in the blaze as we dance

and bang around her, to her, as she whispers
each of our names in night air—through the haze,
we glimpse her face—*Maiden! Mother! Crone!*

Goddess! Goddess! Goddess! Every woman:
past, present, future, blood, brooder, wild
and domestic—*Burn! Burn! Burn!*

*We are Earth! We are Life! We are Noise
and Silence! Burn Yesterday, Today,
and Tomorrow!* Our eyes shut tightly. Wisps

of sweetgrass leave our fingers. In the smoke:
Rise! Rise! Rise with the Moon! escapes our mouths
as we flicker furiously along the treetops.

Mosaic as Time Ends

Split a pomegranate. See the syrup ooze, seeds suspended. Dig in a finger. Paint a black dot on your palm. You are here. The tarot deck falls to the floor. Recognize every face, every type, as yourself. What lives? You live. Thinly spread. Thin as paper. Darkness, but the stars. They twinkle. At the little boys, little girls. They are twinkling. Twelve circle a crown. You have been check-marked, jotted down. The back of your head is in pieces. Particle-small. A feather is collecting each bit of you, piling you on a pillow. There is no explosion, and that's okay. A candle flickers with indifference.

This is everything, happening exactly as it should. The black dot. A blackbird looks down from its nest. It swoops. Down. Down into the dot. Now you. Down into the dot. Hold every part of you. Hold two wands. A wreath. A laurel. Venus, just a marble, packed into your cheek. A fruit with eyes inside. A nest of sun rays. A satin cloak. The dot whirlpools. Everything you are. Everything you could ever be. Spread so thin. Everything becoming nothing. A world entering a pinpoint. You are here. This is you. So thin. Swallow your toes. Your feet. Calves and knees. Thighs. Hips.

Pelvis. Belly. Ribs. Breasts. Shoulders. Forearms. Hands. Swallow the sky. Swallow the trees. Swallow the blackbird. Swallow every sweet sound. Ears. Eyes. Nose. Swallow the stream. Each fish, silver needles in your gums. The stars. The moon. The beetle on your forehead. Skin. Flesh. Everything. Your mother. Your father. Your children. Gas melts solid. Stone falls to cloud. Noise puddles on a tongue. Red roses blaze blue. The darkness is brighter than light. Swallow all. Vacuum-tight. Then swallow your mouth. Have a conversation. Have every conversation you never had.

Acknowledgments

Grateful acknowledgment to the journals in which these poems first appeared, sometimes as earlier versions:

Black Moon Magazine: "American Mosaic"

Bridge Literary Journal: "Standing Over the Great Serpent Mound, 2017"

Delmarva Review: "Song for the Wild Frog"

Ginosko Literary Journal: "Circle Dance," "Daily Rituals," "For John," "Riding into Town," "Sock Hop Love Dance," "The Building," "Thumb Burial," and "Voice from Upstairs"

Gordon Square Review: "At the African American Debutante Ball in Youngstown"

Jenny Magazine: "Backyard Pet Cemetery"

ONE ART: "I Enter Fifty Cemeteries Looking for My Son"

Red Ogre Review: "For Caterpillars"

Sweet Tree Review: "The Fair"

Two Thirds North: "Earning You"

trampset: "Mosaic with Death Approaching"

Dom Fonce works in education, helping adults earn their high school diploma. Dom Fonce lives and writes in Youngstown, Ohio. He is the author of the two chapbooks *Here, We Bury the Hearts* and *Dancing in the Cobwebs*. He holds an MFA from the NEOMFA. His poetry has been published in *trampset, Gordon Square Review, Rappahannock Review, Delmarva Review, Jenny Magazine, Two Thirds North, Sweet Tree Review, Red Ogre Review, Black Moon Magazine, Great Lakes Review,* and elsewhere. Find him at domfoncepoetry.com.

www.ingramcontent.com/pod-product-compliance
Lightning Source LLC
Chambersburg PA
CBHW030055170426
43197CB00010B/1531